First Published 2000 by Pacific Century Publishers
© 2000 Pacific Century Publishers

Photographs © Airphoto International Limited
Kasyan Bartlett
ISBN # 962-217-667-4

Captions: Hilary Binks
Design: Winnie Leung

Pacific Century Publishers Limited

Suite 1603-4, Hon Kwok Jordan Centre, 7 Hillwood Road,
Tsimshatsui, Kowloon, Hong Kong
Tel: (852) 2811 5505   Fax: (852) 2376 2137
Email: airman@airphoto.com.hk

Printed in Hong Kong / China

Hong Kong: Man's Mastery of Nature

Apart from giving it a wonderful harbour, nature was not very kind to Hong Kong and the landscape does not lend itself easily to human habitation. Its 1,092 square kilometres of territory are composed of Hong Kong Island, Kowloon, the New Territories and 235 islands, all with steeply sloping terrain. Add to this the fact that Hong Kong is in the path of the typhoons that sweep across the South China Sea in the summer months and it is hard to understand why the place developed at all.

Yet develop it has. With little flat land available on Hong Kong Island's north shore, reclamation has provided space for commercial growth. Typhoon shelters give protection for both fishing fleets and recreational vessels. The Star Ferry has for over a hundred years linked the Kowloon peninsula with Hong Kong Island. A series of new bridges connects up islands which until recently could only be reached by boat. Nowhere on earth has such an inhospitable landscape been adapted by man with more ingenuity or success.

The Peak

The Peak Tower (above) houses the upper terminus of the famous Peak Tram, which accesses a traditionally exclusive retreat of the wealthy away from the heat and congestion of the city.

Previous pages: **Botanical Gardens** A green oasis in Central, the Botanical and Zoological Gardens were laid out in 1860, five years after the construction of former Government House on the right.

13

Ferries

Despite the modern proliferation of road and rail systems, cross-harbour and inter-island ferries are still the favourite method of transport for many Hong Kong residents and visitors.

Following pages: **Hong Kong Convention & Exhibition Centre** Compared to a soaring bird or a plane lifting off, the spectacular low-rise extension to the Convention Centre is in pleasing contrast with the skyscrapers on the Wanchai waterfront.

Quarry Bay

The majority of Hong Kong residents live in modest high-rise apartments like these at Taikoo Shing and Kornhill, on the north-eastern shore of Hong Kong Island. Quarry Bay was the oldest industrial district in Hong Kong, but has become a thriving residential and office area as land prices have made rentals in Central prohibitive. Luxury townhouses such as those at Stanley (above) are for the affluent minority.

Stanley

The south side of Hong Kong Island boasts some of the territory's most desirable real estate and attractive beaches, such as the one at South Bay (above). Stanley's bustling market is a magnet for tourists.

Following pages: **Repulse Bay** Beautiful, sheltered Repulse Bay got its name from the HMS Repulse, a 19th century pirate chaser which once patrolled the area. Today it is a highly favoured residential area with the Island's most popular beach.

Aberdeen

On the southwest coast of Hong Kong Island, Aberdeen was once a quiet fishing village. Despite recent development, the town remains home to one of Hong Kong's largest fishing fleets, the fishing junks now rubbing shoulders with luxury yachts at the Aberdeen Marina Club. At the foot of the escalator to Ocean Park, Hong Kong's largest entertainment complex on the headland to the left of the typhoon shelter, is the Middle Kingdom (above), a theme village charting 5,000 years of Chinese cultural history.

Tsim Sha Tsui

Perched on the western tip
of the Kowloon peninsula,
in front of green Kowloon
Park, the Gateway complex
overlooks the pier of the
Pacific Club with its
distinctive white roof and
the China Ferry Pier
(above) in the foreground.
To the right are the
Harbour City shopping,
office and hotel complex
and Ocean Terminal, a
venue for visiting ocean
liners.

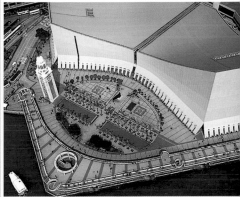

Tsim Sha Tsui

Behind the Kowloon Star Ferry Pier, the original clock tower is all that remains of the Kowloon-Canton Railway terminus, demolished in 1978 to make way for the Cultural Centre (above).

Following pages: **Ocean Terminal** The QEII lies majestically alongside the Ocean Terminal, Hong Kong's main berth for luxury cruise liners.

Hung Hom

The first Cross-Harbour Tunnel, from Causeway Bay on Hong Kong Island to Hung Hom in Kowloon, was built in 1972. Increasing traffic congestion has since necessitated the construction of two further tunnels at the eastern and western ends of the harbour. In front of the red buildings of the Hong Kong Polytechnic University is the square grey roof of the Hong Kong Coliseum, built over the Hung Hom Railway terminus.

Kowloon Peninsula

Severe overcrowding in the southern tip of the Kowloon Peninsula, a mere 12 square kilometres in area, will be relieved somewhat by the availability of new land formed by the West Kowloon Reclamation (top right).

Following pages: **Kowloon Tong** *Nestling beneath the Kowloon Hills, Kowloon Tong is a sprawling residential area characterised by pleasant, low-rise housing along tree-lined roads.*

Kwai Chung

Hong Kong's container port
at Kwai Chung is the
busiest in the world, its
nine terminals handling 15.9
million TEUs, or 20-foot
equivalent units, in 1999.
Containers are discharged
by huge gantry cranes
(above), with the average
ship turn-around time an
amazing 12 hours. Hong
Kong was colonised in
1841 to facilitate trade with
China and trade remains
the territory's lifeblood.

Road Bridges

A vast road, rail and bridge network links Hong Kong's new airport at Chek Lap Kok with the urban areas. The Tsing Ma Bridge (left) leads to the airport, while the Ting Kau Bridge (right) links with the northwest New Territories.

Following pages: **Ting Kau Bridge** Elegant cable-stayed Ting Kau Bridge connects Tsing Yi Island (right) with the northwest New Territories and carries traffic directly into southern mainland China.

Chek Lap Kok

By levelling the island of Chek Lap Kok, off Lantau Island, and reclaiming land from the sea, a platform was made for Hong Kong's new airport in one of the most challenging civil engineering projects in the world.

Following pages: **Hong Kong International Airport** Designed by Sir Norman Foster, the airport passenger terminal and Y-shaped concourse is 1.2 km long and covers 490,000 sq. m. It can handle 35 million passengers and 3 million tonnes of cargo a year.

Shatin

The new town of Shatin, famed for its racecourse (above) where huge sums are wagered at every meeting, is built either side of the Shing Mun Channel, once a naturally flowing river debouching into Tolo Harbour.

Following pages: **The Fanling Golf Club** Top right is the Kowloon-Canton Railway taking passengers to the border crossing at Lo Wu. Shenzhen, China is in the distance.

Nam Sing Wai

The northwest New Territories, near the border with the mainland, is a jigsaw of low-lying fishponds and river channels. The village of Wo Sheng Wai (above) did not sell out to the developers of the nearby Palm Springs residential complex and remains perched on a tiny islet in the middle of the Mai Po Marshes, entirely surrounded by water.

Tolo Harbour

Tolo Harbour in the
northeast New Territories
links the new towns of
Taipo and Shatin with Mirs
Bay. Beyond the island of
Yim Tin Tsai, the Plover
Cove Reservoir was
reclaimed from the sea.
The nearby Sha Lo Tung
Valley (above) is
threatened with
redevelopment.

Following pages: **Fairview
Park** Although farmlands in
the New Territories are fast
shrinking, the residents of
Fairview Park (right) and
Palm Springs (left) still look
out over fields and ponds.

Shenzhen

The meandering Shenzhen
River demarcates the
boundary between the
fishponds of the northern
New Territories of Hong
Kong and the Shenzhen
Special Economic Zone of
the PRC. The Kowloon-
Canton Railway crosses the
border at Lowu (above).
Once an area of rice
paddies, Shenzhen has
undergone a transformation
over the last 20 years and
now displays a scale of
modern high-rise
development
indistinguishable from that
of urban Hong Kong.

Gold Coast

The Gold Coast
development, near the new
town of Tuen Mun in the
northwest New Territories,
boasts a modern hotel
positioned beside a man-
made beach and a marina.
Modern high-rise residential
towers complete the
development. Hong Kong's
superb tropical waters are a
paradise for boating
enthusiasts and yacht
marinas provide moorings
safe from the extremes of
Hong Kong's weather.

Dai Long Wan

Many visitors are surprised to learn that 40% of Hong Kong's land is country parks. The idyllic waters and beaches of the eastern New Territories are inaccessible except to hikers and boaters.

Following pages: **Cheung Chau** Though only 2.4 sq. km. in area, this curious dumbbell-shaped island 12 km southwest of Hong Kong Island has a population of about 40,000 inhabitants, many of whom commute to Hong Kong to work.

Po Lin Monastery

Chinese temples and monasteries were traditionally built in remote and tranquil places. The Po Lin Monastery, located on the beautiful Ngong Ping plateau, southwest Lantau Island, boasts the world's largest seated outdoor bronze Buddha.

Following page: **Kwun Yum Temple** On a quiet hillside in southeast Lantau, this temple was restored by Hong Kong tycoon Li Ka-shing and dedicated to the memory of his wife. Kwun Yum is the Buddhist God of Mercy.

67